Old Mull
Guthrie Hutton

Dougie MacFadyen on his Ferguson tractor and Alan Logan bring in the hay on the croft at Harbour, Ardtun.

www.stenlake.co.uk

ISBN 978-1-84033-379-4

FURTHER READING

British Geological Survey, *The Tertiary Volcanic Districts of Scotland*, 1961.
Currie, Jo, Mull: *The Island and its People*, 2000.
Duckworth, C, & Langmuir, G, West *Highland Steamers*, 3rd edition, 1967.
Faithfull, Joan, *The Ross of Mull Granite Quarries*, 1995.
Hesketh, Barrie, *Taking Off*, 1997.
Le May, Jackie and Gardner, Joanna, *Glen More, a Drive Through History*, 2001.
Maclean-Bristol, Nicholas, *Murder Under Trust*, 1999.
McLeod, Mona Kedslie, *From Charlotte Square to Fingal's Cave*, 2004.
Macnab, Peter, *Highways and Byways in Mull and Iona*, 1988.
Macnab, Peter, *Traditional Tales of Mull*, 1998.
Moir, Peter, & Crawford, Ian, *Argyll Shipwrecks*, 1994.
Ross of Mull Historical Centre, *Discover the Ross*, 2004.
Royal Commission on the Ancient and Historical Monuments of Scotland,
Argyll: An Inventory of the Ancient Monuments, Volume 3, 1980.

ACKNOWLEDGEMENTS

I must thank Mull enthusiasts Bill and Margaret Neithercut for their enormous help both with picture material and in keeping me sustained on my travels. Through them I must also thank Alan Logan for the use of the picture on page 1. I am grateful also to the help given by Fionna Eden-Bushell and Mhairi Dunnings, and to my sister Fiona for putting me up, or should that be putting up with me. My old and drouthy friend Donald Mackinnon was also a great help; a storyteller in the island tradition, he related many tales over a dram which have been woven into this narrative.

Salen looking north in the early 1950s

INTRODUCTION

Mull has a violent past. The land mass was largely formed by the fire and fury of a massive volcano and when the eruptions stopped and the lava cooled a grinding weight of ice reshaped the rocks. Prehistoric habitation sites appear to have been fortified, suggesting the early inhabitants lived in fear, either of their neighbours or wild creatures. Later periods of history are recalled by a folklore that is full of bloodshed and murder as warring clans battled for supremacy. Later, in the nineteenth century, when the clan system had outlived its usefulness, thousands of people were ruthlessly cleared off the land to make way for sheep.

Evidence of this turbulence is everywhere, although time has softened the hard edges to leave a stunningly beautiful island that in recent decades has welcomed a new army of invaders. Tourists have flocked to the island for its solitude, peace and tranquility and to see the rich wildlife, notably golden eagles, sea eagles, otters, whales and dolphins.

Mull is thus a multifaceted island, as rich in natural history as in the history of its people. Although separated from the mainland by only a short sea crossing, that distance is enough to allow Mull to retain its own distinct identity – or should that be identities? While the sheltered east coast is lush, the north and west of the island are much wilder. Glen More, particularly in the wind and rain, feels enclosed and forbidding while the open moors and rocks of the Ross of Mull are more redolent of the windswept Outer Hebrides.

A wide expanse of water may be regarded as a barrier now, but it was not always so. In the days when travelling by land meant a slow and sometimes arduous trudge along undulating, muddy drove roads or packhorse tracks, the sea was an open highway and an island like Mull was at the centre of trading routes. This made the people who could command the waterways very powerful indeed and such power was worth fighting for. Sitting in far-off Edinburgh, the only way Scotland's rulers could maintain a semblance of law and order was to rely on a strong local chief, the Lord of the Isles. These proxy rulers, and their supporters on Mull, while nominally enforcing the authority of the state, were often just a law unto themselves – fighting, feuding and settling scores until time and the outside world caught up with them.

Planned villages began to be imposed on the island in the eighteenth century, a process that met with varying degrees of success, although one of these communities grew to become Tobermory, the island's principal town. With its colourful buildings and superb setting it is now an iconic image for the island, a destination for cruise ships, yacht racers and followers of children's television. The island's attractions are therefore many and varied – even the roads have their fans who use them for an annual car rally (which maybe tells you all you need to know about the quality of Mull's roads!). Mull still thrives on being distinct and different, an island that is close enough to the mainland to be easily accessible, but far enough away to be another world.

Cottages near Bunessan: the upper picture was taken in 1930 at an unknown location, the lower one was photographed in 1949 on the road to Ardtun.

Duart Castle is a wonderful sight. It sits on a prominent headland guarding the entrance to the Sound of Mull inviting ferry passengers to photograph it, but its presence was not always so alluring. The castle was built for war and its commanding presence is a reminder that this part of Scotland was once anything but peaceful. A precise date for its construction is not known, but the building style suggests a 13th century origin with later additions. It was the stronghold of the Macleans, who became the most powerful clan in this part of the inner Hebrides, but fighting and feuding led to an accumulation of debt and the consequent loss of Duart in 1692 to none other than the head of Clan Campbell, the Duke of Argyll. He and his descendants were more interested in the land than the building and by the late nineteenth century it had become a ruin as seen in this picture. In 1911 the Clan Chief, Sir Fitzroy Maclean, bought the castle back from its then owner, Mr Walter Murray Guthrie, and had it restored. The result is a remarkable amalgam of the ancient structure and early twentieth century architecture.

The estate which included the ruined Duart Castle was acquired in the 1820s by Colonel Campbell of Possil. He lived in a two storey Georgian house, but his son John replaced this with a grand mansion, completed in 1858 to the designs of the Edinburgh architect David Bryce. Seven years later, unable to bear the cost of its construction, John Campbell sold the estate to Arbuthnot Charles Guthrie. His successor, Walter Murray Guthrie, returned Duart Castle to Sir Fitzroy Mclean after which the name of the mansion, originally called Duart House, was changed to Torosay Castle. Although it has remained in the family ever since, the burden of maintaining Torosay has never been easy. It was well past its prime when David Guthrie-James inherited in 1945. He had made a name for himself as an adventurer, twice escaping from a POW camp during the Second World War (these exploits were recounted on the television programme *This is Your Life*, which also included a contribution from gamekeeper, Archie MacColl who told of an incident near Lochbuie when the impetuous twelve-year-old David got too close to a golden eagle's nest). When he assumed responsibility for Torosay, David tried running it as a hotel, but when that failed he set about opening it to visitors – a bold move given that, at the time, Mull had few visitors and most of those just wanted to go to Iona. The idea worked and Torosay, with its delightful ornamental gardens, has become one of Mull's principal tourist attractions. It was further enhanced when a miniature railway linking Torosay with Craignure was opened in June 1984.

Craignure became the principal ferry terminal for the island in 1964, when a new pier, which had taken two years to build, was opened. A new boat, *Columba*, also took over the route from the older and smaller *Lochearn*. Ten years later a roll-on roll-off facility was installed alongside; *Caledonia* and *Glen Sannox* operated the route before the purpose-built *Isle of Mull* took over. Before these innovations, getting on or off a steamer at Craignure was something of an adventure. Open boats – one for luggage and the other for people – ferried passengers between the pier and the mail boat. The ferryman apparently never missed a trip, but it could be wet and, if sea conditions were less than calm, could also be tricky. The boat crews helped passengers to catch the right moment to step from one boat to the other as the small one rose and fell alongside the larger vessel, an experience which may have been great fun for the young and fit, but was likely to worry those of more mature years. Such a ferry service must have deterred all but the most intrepid visitors from coming to the island and no doubt did as much to isolate Mull as connect it to the mainland.

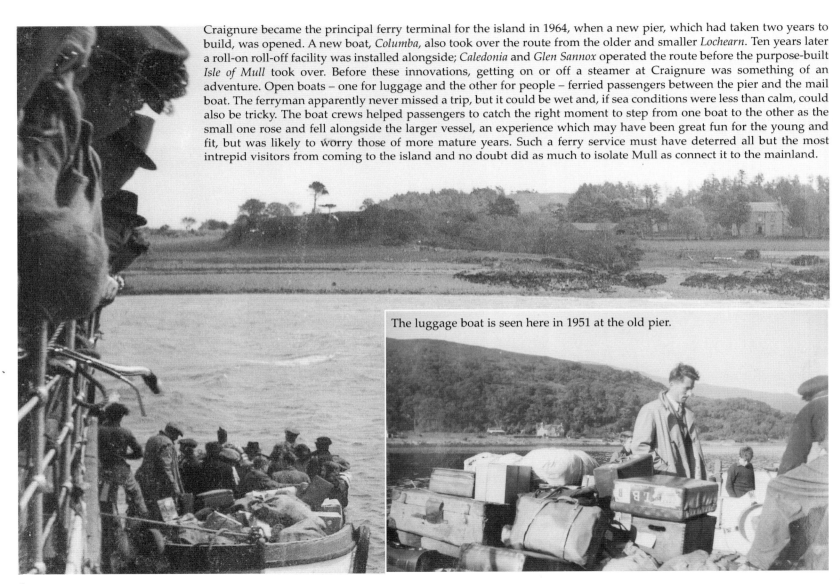

The luggage boat is seen here in 1951 at the old pier.

POST OFFICE, CRAIGNURE.

The new ferry terminal has helped transform Craignure into a substantial community. In the 1920s the post office would have been regarded as more important than the shop that operated alongside, but the opposite is now the case. A ceilidh bar and restaurant was opened in 1988 where the lean-to garage in this picture sits at the side of the post office, although now styled as a roadhouse, bar and bistro its title has more of an international feel. The rough, weedy ground in front is the assembly area for ferry traffic. In former days the nearest hostelry to the old pier was the Craignure Inn, thought to be roughly contemporary with the little Torosay and Kinlochspelve Church nearby. Built in 1783, with a little bellcote surmounting the east gable, it is typical of the small Scots kirk of the time. Kirk and pub coexisted happily side by side, with the scattered community taking advantage of the buildings' proximity to each other by moving from the spiritual sustenance of one to the more earthly fare on offer at the other.

7

Salen Pier was a regular stop for the mail boat between Oban and Mull, but since the building of the new pier at Craignure has fallen into disrepair; the pier buildings are gone, the railings are bent and broken, debris clutters the deck. The pier is seen here in the mid- 1930s with the *Lochinvar* leaving for Tobermory. She was specially built in 1908 for the Oban - Sound of Mull - Tobermory service by Scott's of Bowling, taking over from the paddle steamer *Carabinier*. Only the third ship in MacBrayne's fleet to have a diesel engine, she originally had exhausts rather than the stubby funnel visible here. Although not the prettiest ship in the fleet, she served the route reliably and well for so long she is still fondly remembered. In 1955 she was replaced by the *Lochearn* and for the next five years did excursions and relief work, making her last run between Tobermory and Oban in 1960.

Centrally located with good access to east and west coasts, Salen appears from the map to be the best placed community on the island. Yet it was not created as a settlement until the early 19th century. The village is seen here looking north along the road to Tobermory. Salen Parish Church situated behind the wall and railings on the left was built to the designs of architect William Mackenzie and is dated 1899. The Free Church (in the distance) was built in the early 1880s but is now shorn of its spire and used for private housing. Partly obscured by the tree on the left is the building where the island's only Italian Restaurant is located and beyond that is a prominent house known as the Craig which was formerly a hotel. Just in front of the Craig the road narrows to cross a bridge which was rebuilt subsequent to this picture being taken and is dated 1939.

In 1939 a new bridge was also built over the Aros River. It is just upstream of the old late 18th century bridge (still in use by predestrians) and can be seen in this 1930s photograph. In the 1820s a Polish traveller described Aros as 'a miserable little place consisting of several poor cottages and a rather decent inn', but it has improved since then. On the right of the picture is the ruin of Aros Castle, an ancient pile that could date from as early as the thirteenth century and which was once a stronghold of the Lords of the Isles. The Lordship, a consortium of clans under MacDonald of Islay, ruled over their remote fiefdom in a semi-autonomous way, constantly flouting and irritating the Scottish Crown. James VI resolved to bring the chiefs to heel and in 1608 sent Lord Ochiltree to Aros to meet them. He wined and dined them on board his ship and then set sail, taking the chiefs with him. They remained prisoners of the King until they promised to mend their ways, but once back in their castles carried on much as before.

Aros House was some miles to the north of Aros Castle occupying a superb site overlooking Tobermory Bay from the south. The house was originally built by Hugh Maclean of Coll, but he hit financial problems and had to give up the estate, which was bought in 1874 by Bryce Allan. His fortune had been made in shipping; his Allan Line traded to North and South America and at one time owned a greater tonnage and carried more passengers than either Cunard or the White Star Line.

Bryce Allan died the same year as acquiring Aros and left it to his son, Alexander, who lavished much time, energy and money on developing the estate. He enlarged the house, turning it into a grand Victorian mansion set in magnificent gardens with their own private loch. He also became one of the island's principal benefactors. After the Second World War the property was sold to the Forestry Commission, who demolished the house in 1960. They have since laid out the immediate surrounding area as Aros Park so that everyone can enjoy the splendid view of Tobermory.

Entrance to Bay and Main Street, Tobermory

Tobermory Bay is a superb natural harbour, surrounded on three sides by high ground and protected to the east by Calve Island, seen in the distance of this view across the fisherman's pier. Despite these natural advantages there was no village community to greet a great ship when it dropped anchor in 1588 after the dispersal of the Spanish Armada. At the time Scotland was a neutral country, at war with neither England nor Spain, but Lachlan Mor Maclean of Duart was at war with the Macdonalds and this ship was a potential godsend to him. Instead, therefore, of selflessly assisting these mariners in distress, he tried to use the situation to his own advantage and, in return for providing materials to repair the ship and food for its crew, he obtained the services of 100 Spanish soldiers, armed with firearms and cannon, which he deployed against his foes. Diplomatic circles in Edinburgh thought that Maclean was trying to take possession of the ship and the Spaniards may have thought so too. The atmosphere of tension and distrust which developed may have been the underlying cause of an explosion that ripped the ship apart two months after her arrival causing her to sink with the loss of many lives.

The town itself was established in 1788 by The British Society for Extending the Fisheries and Improving the Sea Coasts of This Kingdom, itself formed two years earlier as an offshoot of the Highland Society of London. It is interesting that no village had been established before, because the anchorage appears to have been well known to seafarers for some time, which is maybe why the Spanish ship found its way to it. This is borne out by two of the most famous visitors to Mull, Dr Samuel Johnson and James Boswell, who arrived in 1773, fifteen years before there was a town. Johnson described the bay as 'the port' and that it had 'a very commercial appearance'. Boswell recorded 12 to 14 vessels from places like Campbeltown, the Clyde and Newcastle lying at anchor. One, returning from Hamburg to Lancaster, was evidence of the harbour being used by vessels trading between west coast ports and the Baltic. He also noted that anything up to 70 ships could be in the bay at any one time.

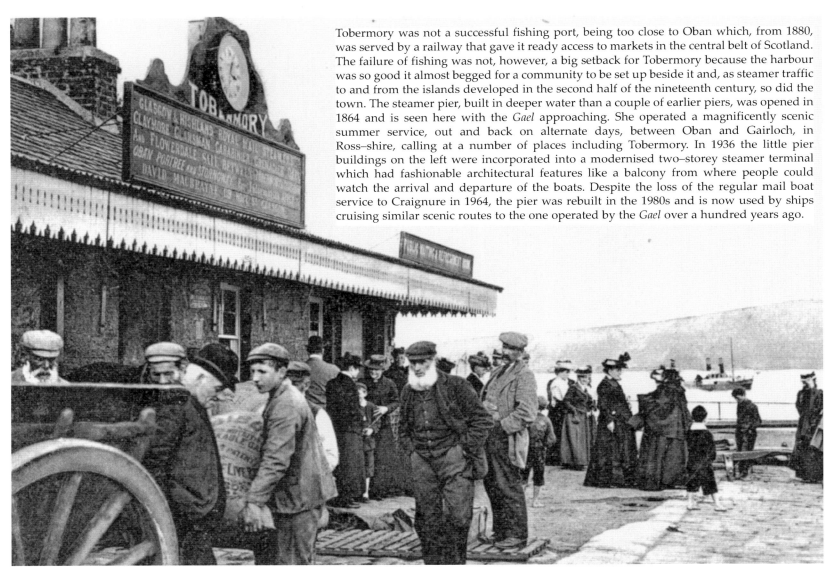

Tobermory was not a successful fishing port, being too close to Oban which, from 1880, was served by a railway that gave it ready access to markets in the central belt of Scotland. The failure of fishing was not, however, a big setback for Tobermory because the harbour was so good it almost begged for a community to be set up beside it and, as steamer traffic to and from the islands developed in the second half of the nineteenth century, so did the town. The steamer pier, built in deeper water than a couple of earlier piers, was opened in 1864 and is seen here with the *Gael* approaching. She operated a magnificently scenic summer service, out and back on alternate days, between Oban and Gairloch, in Ross–shire, calling at a number of places including Tobermory. In 1936 the little pier buildings on the left were incorporated into a modernised two–storey steamer terminal which had fashionable architectural features like a balcony from where people could watch the arrival and departure of the boats. Despite the loss of the regular mail boat service to Craignure in 1964, the pier was rebuilt in the 1980s and is now used by ships cruising similar scenic routes to the one operated by the *Gael* over a hundred years ago.

One of the earlier piers was at the mouth of the Tobermory River, at the area known as Ledaig from which this view of Main Street was taken c.1900. The Free Church building on the left, erected in 1877/78, has been used as a craft and gift shop since the 1960s when the congregation moved into the former United Free Church, which was built in 1910 using the distinctive pink granite from the Ross of Mull. It is separated from the earlier church by the Aros Hall which was gifted to the town by Alexander Allan in the late 19th century, but the indistinct nature of the picture renders it difficult to be certain if either is shown, unlike the Western Isles Hotel standing on its prominent cliff-top site on the right. Erected in 1883 it catered for upmarket steamer passengers, until the Second World War when it welcomed a very different clientele from the Royal Navy, who used Tobermory as a base. Central to the navy's purpose was HMS *Western Isles* which was stationed in the bay to co-ordinate the training of ships' crews in convoy escort duties. Mull itself was a restricted zone and anyone travelling to and from the island had to have a pass.

The little four-windowed building in front of the distillery was built as a Baptist Chapel in 1862. By the end of the eighteenth century John Sinclair, one of the town's early businessmen, was operating a distillery which could have been on the site of the present-day Tobermory Distillery although the date usually given for it being established is 1823. John Hopkins & Company, whose name appears on the gable of the bonded store on the right in this 1904 photograph, took it over in 1890. It was taken over again in 1916 by Distillers Company Ltd, who were forced to close it in 1930 due to unfavourable economic conditions. Renamed Ledaig Distillery it was started up again in 1972 after substantial reconstruction, but the venture struggled and a period of uncertainty followed. The distillery was revived again at the start of the 1990s and taken over in 1993 by Burn Stewart who upgraded it for production of pure malt whisky. The bonded store, sold during the hiatus of the 1970s and 80s, had been converted into flats so the whisky is no longer matured on the island, but taken by road tanker to the mainland where it is stored in casks for ten years before re-emerging as a whisky of remarkable delicacy.

Enjoying the distillery's products will no doubt bring colour to the cheeks of many a happy customer at the bars in the town, but it is Bobby Macleod, accordionist, provost and proprietor of the Mishnish Hotel who tends to get the credit for turning the whole of Main Street into a blaze of colour. The story goes that he took advantage of an offer to try out a new exterior paint and in doing so started a trend. Uniformity and conservatism were discarded as the town's buildings began to appear in increasingly varied and vibrant colours. The result is startling and wonderful and itself inspired the children's television programme Balamory, with its equally colourful characters, to be based around the town. The Mishnish is seen here in in the centre of a picture taken from the steamer pier which also shows the substantial sea wall built to contain the reclaimed ground that forms Main Street.

The shape of the bay and steep slope behind Main Street limited the amount of building at the sea front, so plans were drawn up in the late eighteenth century for the town to develop on the level ground high above. This upper town consisted of a few streets on a grid pattern and was linked to the bay by steeply sloping paths and braes. Some buildings, important to the life of the town, were erected here including the two seen in this view of Argyll Terrace, taken from the site of the present school. On the right is the old school, erected in 1875/6 and now used as the An Tobar Arts Centre. The Parish Church (opened 1897) was built to the designs of Inverness architect John Robertson and replaced the town's first church which had been erected in 1828.

Wireless Telegraph Station, Tobermory

The Parish Church can be seen at the foot of the hill in this view looking down Victoria Street to the bay, the Sound of Mull and beyond to the hills of Morvern. The upper town appears almost serene and orderly compared to the anarchic colour and bustle of the Main Street, but that has not prevented it from being used as the location of some of the Balamory character's houses – Victoria Street is the location of P.C. Plum's House. This is not, however, the area's first association with the world of communications as the wireless telegraphy mast at the west end of Argyll Terrace shows.

Rubha-nan-Gall Lighthouse, to the north of Tobermory, was built in 1857. The actual tower was sited on a small island and linked to the keepers' cottages by a bridge and walkway. The site, at the northern end of the Sound of Mull, at its junction with Loch Sunart and the open sea, has a commanding view of the surrounding area. In the background is Ardnamurchan and out of picture to west (left) is Bloody Bay, so-called because the water is said to have turned red with blood during a sea battle in 1480. This conflict, unusual because most inter-clan warfare took place on land, was fought between the Lord of the Isles, who had MacLean of Duart amongst his loyal supporters, and his son who was seeking to take over the Lordship. The paddle steamer passing the lighthouse in the picture was engaged in the more peaceable business of tourism. David MacBrayne's *Grenadier* operated regularly on the run out of Oban to Staffa and Iona. Regarded as one of the most beautiful vessels in the fleet, she was destroyed by a fire on a September night in 1927 while tied up in Oban.

Glengorm, a grand Victorian mansion in a spectacular setting on the north of the island, was built at the end of the 1850s for James Forsyth of Quinish. There is a story that he intended to name it after the nearby ruin of Dun Ara Castle (see page 38), but changed his mind after an old woman suggested Glengorm, the blue glen. Mr Forsyth, an incomer without the Gaelic, thought it was a nice name without understanding the intended irony that the name would forever be a reminder of the blue smoke of the burning crofts cleared to create the estate. Perhaps just a story, it reflects the reality that Glengorm is associated with that prolonged period of the nineteenth century, the Highland Clearances, when landlords evicted tenants they regarded as unproductive from the land and replaced them with sheep. The evictions came later to Mull than the better known Clearances in Sutherland, but they were every bit as harsh. The potato famine of 1846 appears to have been one of the principal triggers when smallholders (crofters) were unable to feed themselves and faced starvation. People were forced off the land by increased rents and left the island for the New World or the growing towns and cities of the central belt of Scotland.

Before the end of the eighteenth century on Mull there were clusters of cottages, but nothing that would be recognised today as a village or town. Those places that fit such a label, including Tobermory, were deliberately created by landowners or others. Dervaig is no exception, having been founded by Alexander MacLean of Coll in 1799. Initially consisting of 26 paired cottages arranged along a single street, Dervaig has evolved into perhaps the most picturesque village on the island and has changed little over the last hundred years or so. The view here is from the Bellachroy Hotel, which claims to be the oldest inn on the island, predating the building of Dervaig. In the distance the fine nineteenth century house known as Oakfield acts as a splendid visual terminal for the main street.

The view from behind Oakfield is no less compelling with the Bellachroy Hotel providing a complementary terminal at its end of the street. Beyond the hotel and just out of the picture on the right is Kilmore Parish Church. It has a distinctive round tower, a feature redolent of similar towers in Ireland. Although this makes the church look like an ancient structure, and it did replace an earlier building dating from the 1750s, the church was only built in 1905, to the designs of architect Peter McGregor Chalmers. Beyond the church (and therefore even further out of the picture) is the location of the Mull Little Theatre, started in 1966 by Marianne and Barrie Hesketh. Their shows were staged in a converted byre and the Heskeths did everything from acting and changing the scenery to selling the tickets and refreshments. The venture achieved fame as the smallest theatre in the world, but in 1984 fate intervened when Marianne died from cancer and Barrie subsequently left the island. However, in the grand tradition of 'the show must go on' the little theatre they started is still in existence.

In the mid-eighteenth century there was a short-lived plan to grow flax at Penmore for the linen trade, but the existing Penmore Mill (now used for holiday accommodation), to the west of Dervaig, is thought to date from the 19th century. Plentiful rain has given Scotland, and Mull in particular, an abundant supply of renewable energy in the form of fast flowing rivers and burns which were harnessed in many places to drive mills, mainly for grain. To justify the large investment of building them a system known as thirlage was introduced by which landowners tied, or thirled, their tenants to the mill. The tenants had to help with the mill's upkeep, use it to grind their corn and desist from using other means of milling. They also had to give some of their grain to both the landlord and the miller, who often became a social outcast because of suspicions that he gave back short measure.

Quinish was Maclean country, but it was not Duart who held these lands it was Maclean of Coll. The two families quarrelled over who owed whom allegiance which, as these things tended to do, led to murder and mayhem. In this the Coll MacLeans seem to have been at a disadvantage because they had no castle or stronghold on Mull and in times of conflict had to defend their interests out in the open. This kind of inter-clan violence had stopped providing material for the bards to embellish long before Quinish House was built about 1810. Originally it was a simple structure taking in the three windows facing the camera here, but was later extended on both sides with the additions of the turreted wing on the right and the simpler one on the left. One of its owners, James Forsyth, also built Glengorm Castle, but before he could move into his new mansion he fell from his horse and broke his neck, thus fulfilling a prophesy that he would see the house completed, but never live in it. Lairds involved in the Clearances elsewhere received similar threats before their accidental deaths, so these coincidences are perhaps not always what the storytellers would have us believe, but they make for good stories.

CROAIG HOUSE & PIER

Croig, a delightful spot on a north-facing inlet has changed little outwardly since this picture was taken about a century ago, except that the inn is now a private house and the slip pier no longer resounds to the clatter of hoofs. Cattle heading for mainland markets from the islands off Mull's north west coast were landed at Croig from where they were driven across the island to the piers at Grass Point or Croggan. This part of the north coast of Mull is called Mornish and people have been attracted to it for centuries, because it is almost littered with archaeological remains. These include a standing stone, cairns and about a fifth of the fortified sites on Mull, three of which Dun nan Gall, Dun Guaire and a small fort on Eilean nan Gobhar are within a short distance of Croig. They all use natural features such as a cliff, a promontory or an island for their strength. There are many other ancient sites across Mull, giving the island a rich prehistoric heritage to complement its more recent history.

Calgary has one of the finest sandy beaches in Mull, attracting numerous tourists in the summer. It is seen here from the pier, a simple stone structure which has been modified and extended using pink granite from the quarries on the Ross of Mull. It is on the north side of the bay, just to the seaward side of a prominent geological feature, a whinstone dyke. The pier itself has entered Mull's folklore as the last land trodden by people leaving this part of the island during the Clearances, never to return. The pier was also used by boats taking sheep to and from the Treshnish Islands. In a westerly wind, common in these parts, it was very exposed and so those ubiquitous go anywhere, carry anything, cargo vessels of the west coast, the puffers, preferred to beach on the sand and move off when the incoming tide refloated them. Puffermen were also known to like strong drink, as did Calgary folk who used nearby caves to distil illicit whisky.

Calgary Castle is a large mansion tacked on to an eighteenth century house which itself was built on earlier structure. The ornate castellated frontage dates from 1817 and is seen here in the 1930s with infilled window openings and the marks of where a conservatory once butted onto the building. The gardens were known for their rhododendrons and exotic plants. Calgary also gained recognition for a stud of Highland ponies, but while these have brought a degree of notice, the name has become famous thanks to James Farquarson Macleod. A native of Skye, he was a staying at the castle in 1872 when he received a summons to take up a position in the newly formed North West Mounted Police in Canada (later the Royal Canadian Mounted Police). Three years later he took charge of a badly run and mutinous fort in Alberta and renamed it Fort Calgary, after the place in Mull where his adventure began. This fort and the adjacent settlement have since grown into the modern city of Calgary. The old castle was back in the news in 2003 when pop star Midge Ure of Ultravox, Live Aid and Live 8 fame was married there.

Storytelling, where fact and fiction are creatively entwined, is a delightful feature of Gaelic culture. A story, with more than one version, is told of Ailean na Sop the bastard son of Maclean of Duart and the heiress of Torloisk. Her later husband resented the boy and caused him to run away by scalding his hand with hot food. The boy grew into a young man who acquired a fearsome reputation as a sea rover. One day he parked his galleys in Loch Tuath and came to visit his mother, but she had died and her cruel husband had inherited Torloisk. He welcomed the young pirate and persuaded him that he could enrich himself by going to the island of Ulva, killing the resident chief, Macquarie, and taking over from him. The rover landed with murder on his mind, but the old man received him as a guest and, while entertaining him with food and drink, reminded him of his treatment as a boy. With his memory of past injustices thus stirred, Ailean na Sop returned to Mull, killed his stepfather and took over Torloisk instead. The house (*left*), seen here c. 1905, reflects none of this brutal past being an eighteenth century mansion enlarged and embellished at various times through the nineteenth century. Ulva had ceased to be Macquarie territory before in the early nineteenth century Ulva House (*right*) was erected. After a fire in 1953 it was replaced by a similar structure which incorporated some of the old building.

The small community of Gruline, on the west side of the narrow neck of land that joins the north of the island to the south, is cut off from the shore by the meandering course of the River Ba, said to be Mull's finest salmon river. A tributary of the Ba flows to the north of this house, where the post office was located. Formerly known as Glenforsa Post Office, it was set up by 1898 and operated in a corrugated iron lean-to (which has since been removed) until its closure in 1965. The building sits across the road from St Columba's Episcopal Church which dates from 1874. Gruline's main claim to fame, however, is as the former home of the man regarded as the father of Australia, Major-General Lachlan Macquarie. His name became familiar to me when my family emigrated to Australia and, as a young Scot, I felt some pride when I learned about the part he had played in the history and development of that great country.

Australia, or more exactly New South Wales, was established as a penal colony in 1788 and policed by soldiers of the New South Wales Corps. The names of the first four Governors – Philip, Hunter, King and Bligh (of the Bounty!) – are etched on my memory from school history lessons. They were all naval men who were unable to control the soldiery and the colony's descent into corruption and criminality. All that changed when the New South Wales Corps was disbanded and Macquarie, with his regiment of Highland soldiers, arrived in 1809. He was the first military Governor and established law and order, setting the country on the path to what it is today. Macquarie came from an Ulva family and in 1804 acquired Gruline House, the little building on the right, not the big house with the round tower (which built in the 1860s). Macquarie's duties left him little time to spend at Gruline, but he is credited with establishing Salen as a community. He died in 1824 and his mausoleum on Gruline Estate is managed for the National Trust of Australia (New South Wales) by the National Trust for Scotland.

During their visit to Mull in 1773 Dr Samuel Johnson and James Boswell travelled across the island on horseback to Ulva Ferry, a journey through a landscape which Johnson described as a 'gloom of desolation'. His discomfort was no doubt shared by the poor wee pony that had to bear his considerable weight over the wet and difficult ground. The two men spent the night on Ulva, before travelling on to Inch Kenneth where Dr Johnson was apparently delighted to see cart tracks as evidence that roads and civilisation had penetrated the Hebrides. The journey between the two islands was made by boat, which let the travellers see the formidable Gribun cliffs without having to journey round them by land, if indeed a path existed at that time. The 1,000 feet high cliffs, in effect the western slopes of Ben More, drop sharply to the shore and would have presented a difficult rock-strewn route although, as this picture shows, a road had been formed around their base by the 1920s. Scant improvement since then might prompt a latter-day Dr Johnson to make equally caustic comments about Mull's roads.

In July 1930 the 63rd Edinburgh Troop of Boy Scouts were trekking across Mull to Iona. They made it safely round the Gribun cliffs, but as they ascended the slope to Gleann Seilisdeir, they encountered a landslide above Balmeanach which threatened to disrupt their progress. Boy Scouts, however, are taught to be resourceful, show initiative, and have a spirit of adventure, so undaunted they dismantled their trek cart and portaged it and all their equipment around the obstacle. Doubtless they looked on it as a challenge, and it probably never entered their heads to consider the kind of health and safety implications that might attend such a dilemma today. Mull's connections with Scouting are, of course, very strong because Sir Charles H. F. Maclean of Duart, 'Chips', as he was known, was Chief Scout of the Commonwealth.

With their adventure at Balmeanach behind them, the Scouts are seen here with their reassembled trek cart at Pennyghael. The boys set up camp close to the Leidle River, where they found a pool in which to swim. Even in July the water would have been cold – Scouts were expected to be tough and hardy too. They were also taught First Aid, although it is not known if the Edinburgh boys were aware of Pennyghael's associations with medicine. A cairn and cross, just to the west of the village, commemorates the Beatons, sixteenth century doctors who were practised in the use of herbs. They originally came from France and such was their skill that they became physicians to the Lords of the Isles and the Macleans of Duart; even King James VI in Edinburgh recognised their ability. So alas did some rivals whose remedy for an acute attack of envy was to poison John Beaton, the member of the family who had so impressed the king.

Our trekking Scouts took this picture when they climbed Ben More, an impressive mountain which rises to 3,169 feet above sea level, a height that makes it a Munro (a single peak over 3,000 feet) and the only one in the Hebrides outwith Skye. Ben More was shaped by volcanic action, but is not an old volcano even though it looks like one. The volcano that shaped the whole mass of the island south of Saline and Gruline was much bigger than just one mountain. Active for millions of years, over time it moved from south east to north west creating two vast calderas, lava-filled basins surrounded by dykes. These were penetrated by a number of explosion vents which forced masses of rock upwards, creating the chaotic landscape of which Ben More is part. The lavas from these eruptions spread in layers to shape the island's landscape and nowhere is this clearer and more dramatic than on the Burg, the headland owned and managed by the National Trust for Scotland. It includes the imprint of a tree, fossilised when it was caught in a lava flow some 63 million years ago and discovered in the 1820s by geologist John McCulloch.

Bunessan was established as a crofting and fishing community by the 5th Duke of Argyll. He held the title from 1770 to 1806 and was a noted agricultural improver as well as a man who took seriously the responsibilities imposed on him by ancient clan loyalties. The Duke also tried to establish a similar settlement further west, at Kintra, but while it remained small, Bunessan grew into the largest village on the Ross of Mull. The picture shows the view from the village, looking east to Ben More, in the late 1930s. The school building, erected in 1869, is on the right with the war memorial just visible to its left. As well as a school the village supported a mill, a hotel (the Argyll Arms), and two churches. The Church of Scotland was built in 1804 in the centre of the village by a local mason to serve the parishes of Kilfinichen and Kilvickeon. The Baptist Church was built in 1891 with locally quarried granite.

The earliest structure in the village is probably the Argyll Arms, the oldest part of which dates from 1790. The building, which can be seen on the right of the lower picture, has changed shape and size over the years, most recently when it was extended in the 1960s. It appears to have been set up as a hostelry to cater for passing travellers and, if some local opinion is to be believed, as an attempt by the Duke of Argyll to control the consumption of illicit whisky. Originally the main road through Bunessan was the one that cuts up behind the Argyll Arms to Uisken, but in the late 1930s the track in front of the hotel, to and from the deep water pier, was made into the main road.

Bunessan was also a regional shopping centre with a number of stores, some of which can be seen here. One of the most remarkable shops operated in the building in the left foreground of the upper picture (now the site of the fire station) and was run by the MacQuarrie family, who also traded with a boat from the small pier behind the shop. They took produce to coastal locations and some of the islands in an operation that sounds like an aquatic version of door-to-door sales vans.

Bunessan Pier, sited to the west of the village, was built in 1846 as one of a number of schemes designed to provide work for men who received food supplies as relief from the potato famine that gripped the west of Scotland at the same time as the better known famine in Ireland. The pier became an important element in transport links between Glasgow and the Western Isles. One of its main users was the boat in the picture, *Dunara Castle*, named after an ancient fort or castle site on the north of Mull near Glengorm. She set out on her maiden voyage in 1875 and continued in service for over 70 years, taking time out for occasional refits, one of which, in 1894, changed her appearance by replacing her two original funnels with one. Her service was also interrupted by unexpected events, such as taking part in the 1930 evacuation of St. Kilda. In March 1947 she ran aground on the rocks at Bunessan, but was refloated after a week and continued her journey. Less than a year later, in January 1948, she made her last journey to the isles and went to the breaker's yard in June of that year.

Under the 5th Duke of Argyll's benign rule the population on the Ross of Mull increased and usable land was divided amongst many more people, creating plots which were hardly big enough to be viable, even in the good times. It was a potentially dangerous situation for the crofters who, in the 5th Duke's successors, had landlords with other priorities. The 6th Duke preferred a hedonistic lifestyle, incurring huge debt which the 7th Duke inherited along with the title in 1839. A sick man, he died eight years later leaving the 8th Duke to deal with the estate's financial problems and the crisis caused by the failure of the potato harvest in 1846. A bright young man with political ambitions, he left the day-to-day management of the estate on Mull to a newly appointed factor, John Campbell of Islay, who lived midway between Bunessan and Fionnphort at Ardfenaig House which looks suitably deserted in this view across Loch Caol. He was also known as Factor Mor (the big factor) and for many tenants he was big trouble. It may not have seemed so at first as he set in train a number of projects to provide work in return for meal, such as the building of Bunessan Pier, but crofters who failed to work or to heed his entreaties to grow more food found themselves with a one-way ticket off the island. Factor Mor's harsh regime is still spoken of with dread.

Ferrying between the Ross of Mull and Iona was a somewhat ad hoc affair until the mid-nineteenth century when the need to get the mails through led to a formalised service and the construction of slip piers. Sailing skiffs operated up to the mid-1920s when similar, clinker-built, motor driven boats took over. Harbour launches, including *Craignure*, the boat that had previously ferried passengers between the jetty and *Lochinvar* at Craignure, operated the route at different times until 1979 when Caledonian MacBrayne put the new car ferry *Morvern* on the crossing. She was replaced in 1992 by the purpose–built *Loch Buie*.

Once established as the ferry terminal, Fionnphort began to grow. Fishing developed and the quarrying industry moved in, attracted by the area's pink granite, ancient rock which the lavas flowing from the volcanoes to the east did not cover. The principal quarry was at Tormore to the north of Fionnphort, but other sources were also worked, including erratic boulders like the one seen here on the beach. The split in the rock was, according to popular theory, made in the 1870s by quarrymen, but the Duke of Argyll (a keen amateur geologist) stopped them from doing any more damage to this important feature. Another story tells of the quarry manager, who had a wicked sense of fun, splitting the rock as a present for his granddaughter on her fourth birthday.

Ross of Mull granite was admired not just for its appearance, but was also favoured by builders and engineers for its strength. On Erraid, the tidal island off the south west tip of the Ross, a quarry was opened to provide stone to build the lighthouse on Dubh Artach, a small but dangerous rock islet that sticks up above the surface of the sea about fifteen miles to the south. Thomas and David Stevenson were commissioned to build the light which was begun in 1867 and completed five years later. The houses built for the quarrymen and construction workers were then used as a shore station for the Dubh Artach lighthouse keepers and from 1892 for those manning the Skerryvore light also. The houses and quarry are seen here looking across at the island from Fidden. In 1952 the shore station was moved to Oban and the houses were sold to the Findhorn community. Erraid also featured in Robert Louis Stevenson's novel *Kidnapped* as the island where the hero of the story, David Balfour, came ashore after the ship he had been imprisoned on was wrecked. This was no coincidence; Robert is known to have visited his father, Thomas Stevenson, on Erraid during construction of the lighthouse.

A prehistoric dun, standing stones and the remains of houses emptied by the Clearances combine to create a picture of the area around Uisken as one which has seen more human activity in the past than the present. That the process is continuing seems to be borne out by comparing this picture from the 1930s with the present day. The little cottage in the foreground, with its trim thatched roof and brave white-painted walls, has gone although the cottage beyond is still there. Despite all the activity that the area appears to have supported, there was no made-up road to Bunessan (only a couple of miles away) until one was built by local people, in return for meal given out as relief, at the the time of the 1840s potato famine. Roads and other aspects of infrastucture are taken almost for granted these days, but at that time improvements such as this were funded out of the income from the estate. Landowners were, in effect, the local authority and when tenants could not afford demands for higher rents they were forced off the land.

This picture from a c.1905 postcard also shows a level of human activity that has since declined to almost nothing. It is entitled Port Uisken, a name that implies something more substantial than a beach, and at this time appears to have been well used. Today a couple of mooring lines stretched out to sea point to some usage, but there are no boats drawn up on the sand, no fishing nets and the little thatched cottage is a roofless ruin.

Fishing was actively encouraged as part of the process of weaning crofters off the subsistence farming that had been found so cruelly wanting with the crop failures. The road to Bunessan was expected to provide access to markets without the need for small boats to risk a journey in rough seas around the Ross to sell their catch. On the evidence of this picture, that aspiration seems to have been partly met, at least up to the early 1900s.

Carsaig, like Uisken, is at the end of a long, narrow road, this time heading south from Pennyghael through Glen Leidle. Near the end of the road is a lonely telephone box which achieved fame as a location in the 1945 feature film *I Know Where I'm Going*, one of a number of films shot partly on Mull which include *When Eight Bells Toll*, *The Eye of the Needle* and *Entrapment*. Mull has many old, red, cast-iron telephone boxes and the notices stuck on them proclaiming the arrival of Broadband just add to the charm. A tale is told of one erected by Post Office engineers during dry summer weather – when it rained, the adjacent stream became so swollen that no-one on the phone could hear anything above the roaring torrent.

The now disused pier at Carsaig was erected in the 1850s with the intention of encouraging the fishing industry, but Carsaig is best known for its geology, with these majestic cliffs leading round the coast to the extraordinary columnar basalt formations known as the Carsaig Arches. Artists have also been going to Carsaig since the 1960s when a summer school of painting was started at Inniemore Lodge, a house dating from 1877 and seen here in 1951.

The prolonged volcanic activity that created southern Mull and Ben More was followed by an equally protracted ice age when the once molten rocks were scoured into new shapes by slowly-moving glaciers. The principal feature created by this process is Glen More which has provided generations of Muileachs (Gaelic for people from Mull) with a route across the south of the island. Initially an informal path, the road evolved over time into a drove road and then a made-up highway which, despite upgrading, is barely adequate for the massive tour buses that trail along it to one of Scotland's premier tourist attractions, although before the advent of the new car ferry the local bus was one of the few vehicles on the road. The bus provided many vital services: people who wanted something in Oban would leave a note and the money under a stone beside the road and the driver would deliver it to the ferry at Craignure; the required item would be on the return ferry and duly delivered to the roadside by the bus driver the next day. The driver also knew where he could stop the bus for a moment to check the traps he had set to catch rabbits and other game.

The flat alluvial land at Lochbuie has attracted human activity for thousands of years, with a cairn, standing stones and a stone circle situated behind this house and castle. The two buildings were, at different times, residences of the Maclaines, a branch of Clan Maclean with a penchant for self-destruction which allowed Duart to assert superiority. There is certainly a forbidding aura about Moy Castle (on the right), a gaunt and semi-ruinous structure sitting on a rock outcrop above a beach blackened with basaltic sand. Parts of it could date from the fourteenth century and later additions have been made, possibly up to the seventeenth century. A constant supply of natural spring water was incorporated into the structure and it also had (perhaps still has!) a ghost said to be that of the chief's son who, nagged by his wife, engaged in a fight with his father during which he literally lost his head. His restless spirit is said to ride furiously around the castle whenever a death in the family is imminent.

In the mid-18th century the family built a new house adjacent to the castle and it was here that Dr Johnson and Boswell spent their last night on Mull in 1773. They enjoyed the old chief's gruff, eccentric company, but were not greatly impressed by the house which was replaced twenty years later by the Georgian mansion on the left of the picture.

To appreciate the awesome scale of the Mull volcano, look at a map of the island from a distance and focus on the shape of the land and the lochs in the south east: Loch Buie, Loch Uisg and Loch Spelve. These huge blocks of land and water have a distinctly curving shape, radiating out from a centre, the centre of the volcanic activity. It gives Loch Spelve an unusual alignment for a sea loch, running in line with the shore for five miles and only linked to the open sea by an inlet where Croggan Pier is located. The pier was used by farming folk to ship animals to Oban, but despite its sheltered site was less used than Grass Point which was closer to the mainland. This was always a dangerous coast for shipping; the magnetic pull of the mountains gave false compass readings which lured a number of vessels onto the remote, precipitate shore. Although no lives were lost in either incident, it happened twice in January 1958 when the boom defence vessel *HMS Barcombe* ran aground near the entrance to Loch Buie and two days later the puffer *Glenrosa* piled onto the rocks alongside.

Auchnacraig Post Office was renamed Lochdon in 1965, an unremarkable event for a community that had once been at the centre of a religious storm. In 1843 ministers and parishioners left the Church of Scotland in great numbers to set up the Free Church of Scotland. The issue that caused this schism struck at the heart of Presbyterianism, the quesion of who had the right to appoint a minister – a powerful patron or the congregation as a whole. Those who remained with the established church did everything they could to stifle the upstart church, but this just made the latter more determined and more convinced they were right. The community of Lochdonhead on Mull became a symbol of the struggle. Banned by Colonel Campbell of Possil from meeting anywhere on his estate, they met in a tent set up in a gravel quarry on the shore between high and low water mark. The Colonel's doomed struggle to defend the established order may well have been a factor in his early death. The Free Church building was erected near the gravel pit in 1852. At the time schools were often run by the church. Many teachers, including the one at Lochdon, left to join the Free Church ranks, but the need to educate children remained and so the little school rode out the storm and is now Lochdonhead Primary School.